Sahara

10

Aozou

Zouar is approached across a plain; Bardai down a palm-fringed gorge; on to Aozou one drops from the sky. The road keeps to the mountains until the last possible moment, leading to the brink of a precipice at the foot of which, a thousand feet below, lies the village. To anyone gazing down from above, the crowns of the close-packed palms merge into an unbroken expanse of emerald green, from beneath which there emerges a thin stream of that same salty precipitation that gives its name to the *Trou au Natron* – a sinister reminder that all the Tibesti is volcanic and that even here, deep in the ground beneath this smiling little oasis, all is not well.

From the start Aozou struck us as being a happy sort of place. Being considerably more remote even than Bardai it hardly ever sees a foreigner, and our appearance threw it into a state of excitement far greater than that which we normally expected to arouse. As usual we drove straight to the fort to notify the authorities of our arrival; and when we emerged a few minutes later we found every child in the village, male and female, and a fair admixture of the adult population as well, gathered round the Land Rovers. Every face was quick with expectation, determined not to miss an instant of the free entertainment we were offering. To begin with this entertainment must have struck many of them as a bit of a let-down; it certainly seemed one to me when the lieutenant in charge, like his opposite number in Zouar, insisted on taking us on a conducted tour of his vegetable garden. By this time we had all of us inspected a good many Sahara vegetable gardens of one kind or another, and the novelty of picking our way between soggy irrigation ditches, murmuring, '*Ah, les belles tomates*' at regular intervals, had begun to pall; we bore up as best we could, but it was a relief to us all when our guide returned us to the starting-point and said, '*Maintenant il faut chercher un beau site pour votre camp.*' This, in fact, seemed to be the moment the crowd had been waiting for. With much laughter, occasionally interspersed with loud falsetto whoops of joy, they surrounded the lieutenant and ourselves and accompanied us to a spot on the edge of the palm-grove, beside a little running stream, where it was generally agreed that we should be most comfortable. Then, forming

74. Hospitality on the road to Aozou

themselves into as tight a circle as our own activities permitted, they settled down to watch.

Sooner or later on our travels, we nearly all of us run up against the problem of the uninhibited onlookers – usually in the form of a group of peasants who appear from nowhere at the start of a picnic, take up a position a yard or two away and then, refusing all offers of food themselves, follow every mouthful with their eyes until the meal is over. Even at picnics this technique can be unnerving enough; but at a night camp, where there are no tents to afford the minimum of privacy and not even any bushes for cover, it can become a serious matter, and never have I known it to attain such formidable proportions as that evening at Aozou. The crowd at the start must have numbered at least forty – forty pairs of staring, unblinking eyes, missing nothing, examining every item we drew from our kitbags, taking in our every move. As we worked on and their fascination increased, they became more serious; slowly their laughter died, then even their conversation. Never, I should emphasise, was there anything remotely hostile about them; they were perfectly friendly – just very, very curious.

Our own reactions varied between agonised embarrassment and stoic fortitude. None of us felt like asking them, in so many words, to go away; such a request would, we feared, be thought exceedingly impolite, and the last thing we wanted was to cause offence. I argued furthermore that inconveniences of this kind were part and parcel of travelling – that the further afield one ranged the greater the attention one was bound to attract, and that one must simply resign oneself to it just as one did to any other discomfort. All that was needed, anyway, was patience. Sooner or later our audience was bound to get bored and wander off. No, I was told, this was insensate optimism. Were not the Toubou famous for their staying power? If strong action were not taken nobody would be able to undress at all; meanwhile there were other needs that were even more pressing. I looked round; they were quite right. One or two of the older spectators had indeed slipped away; but the hard core that remained, consisting almost entirely of children and adolescents, clearly had no thought of departure. They had on the contrary decided that a long vigil lay ahead, and they were even now digging themselves in for the night.

At last Costa took the matter in hand. 'Then,' he said, 'if they are looking for entertainment, that is what we must give them. Then they will be satisfied and go away.' We looked doubtful. Would not any form of entertainment we could offer simply whet their appetite for more? Besides, what could we possibly do to amuse them? But Costa, delighted at his idea and by now looking forward hugely to his own performance, was not to be shaken. Delving into his kitbag, he extracted some colourful garment, twisted it expertly into a funny hat and put it on. Then, trousers rolled up to the knee, he began to dance; and as he danced he sang:

> *Y avait dix filles dans un pré,*
> *Toutes les dix à marier,*

75. The rocks near Bardai

76. (overleaf) Zouar – the dance

DATE DUE

5-15-70			
GAYLORD			PRINTED IN U.S.A.